POEMS

*(Reflections and Ruminations
Observations and Inspirations)*

RICK PAULSEN

Order this book online at www.trafford.com
or email orders@trafford.com

Most Trafford titles are also available at major online book retailers.

Print information available on the last page.

ISBN: 978-1-4907-7727-6 (sc)
ISBN: 978-1-4907-7728-3 (e)

Trafford rev. 10/21/2016

Trafford
PUBLISHING®   www.trafford.com

North America & international
toll-free: 1 888 232 4444 (USA & Canada)
fax: 812 355 4082

To my family for all their encouragement
and support. Especially Kathy.

Contents

THE HIGHS AND LOWS OF A POET

Writing is my avocation
I like words and their derivation
find pleasure in a conjugation
I read them with much admiration
without words no conversation
or literary innovation
I study them with fascination
look them up for edification
practice their enunciation
so in my humble estimation
if there were an award citation
for using one's imagination
in the use of word manipulation
I might get a nomination
because with little provocation
and always with anticipation
I start a poetic fabrication
a sometimes lengthy dissertation
from some deep mind exploration
or just a random observation
which can cause exasperation
as I struggle in frustration
to complete a new narration
an oft time wordy enumeration
that if well done needs no translation
to understand my inspiration
then offer it with reservation
for review and examination
hoping for a commendation
from which I'd feel exhilaration
a very pleasant high sensation
almost instant gratification
and that for me is compensation
but the high is of short duration

then I need new stimulation
and panic at the affirmation
that I am facing total stagnation
at loss to start a new creation
I'm lower than a balloon's deflation
as I search in desperation
for subjects needing clarification
that will start a new collocation
then once an idea is in formation
I work and work with determination
and can't escape its rumination
until I achieve its vocalization
so let me say this in summation
I think that I might need sedation
my brow is damp with perspiration
and I'm suffering dehydration
I'm weak as if from heat prostration
my head aches from the concentration
and is spinning in rotation
please someone get me exhortation
rid me of this aberration
my wife then smiles with adoration
and says, "just for your information
I think you need a long vacation"
bingo! that lights a spark of activation
I think there's a poem in that allegation
I can't ignore the strong temptation
to start another oration
hoping for the next ovation
so on and on goes this fixation
highs and lows in elevation
I guess there'll never be salvation
until I face the realization
like a word play on a "Stones" quotation
"I just can't get no relaxation."

HARBINGER OF HOPE

For Kathy
8/2013

Look out the window on a bleak winter day
to a bitter cold north wind.
Feel the chill to the depth of your soul
it seems it might never end.

This season of darkness goes on forever
how we wish it would just go away.
Almost too much for a body to bear
how we long for a bright sunny day.

This is the time when the sun shines the least
clouds and dark skies prevail.
We can't see the light, can't feel right
held captive in winter's jail.

So it might be hard to remember
that winter always turns to spring.
Flowers, birds and sunny skies
a truth on which to cling.

The seasons are a metaphor
for troubles to be shed.
Like winter always yields to spring
there are sunny days ahead.

MAGNOLIODEAE

Pity the fallen Magnolia tree
crushed by the toppling of the ash
in the summer storm some weeks ago
when a fearsome wind from the west did blow
ravishing so much in its path.

The Magnolia stood for many years
fifty for sure and maybe more.
Now all that remains is the lonely stump
gone the branches and the trunk
bare the earth from which they were tore.

With flowers pink and leaves of green
with branches drooping to the ground
it proclaimed that spring was here to stay
that summer's warmth was on the way
the change from winter quite profound.

It makes me sad that the tree is gone
but look and see what think I see.
Small green sprouts have now appeared
around the stump when the tree was cleared.
Is the tree's rebirth soon to be?

I'm convinced the tree will stand again.
Come back better than before.
Shaking off that bitter wind
growing strong its branches will extend
ever skyward they will soar.

Pity for this Phoenix tree?
No, more a lesson to be had.
If your roots are deep and strong
you can overcome when things go wrong
find inner strength when times are bad.

UNIVERSAL WONDER

What a wonder it is to me. The night sky.
As through my telescopic lens I spy.
I look, there is so much to see.
In the heavenly bodies up so high.
How could this all have come to be?

The skeptic lurking in my soul
questions a Creator's roll.
In making this glorious spectacle
of which I seek to learn is my goal.
Yet it truly is a miracle.

What a wonder it is to me. The sky at night.
Filled with a billion stars so bright.
Galaxies, comets and constellations galore.
As I gaze into the heavens tonight
I look, I search and I explore.

This must be how Vincent felt
when with awe I stare at Orion's belt.
On that starry night he was inspired
and the touch of his brush the canvas felt.
Creating a work that's so admired.

Could this really just be happenstance?
So many stars at a glance.
Again I doubt it can be so.
It really can't just be by chance.
The sights the dark night does bestow.

So here I am still in doubt
as to how this all has come about.
I guess I'll just enjoy the site
instead of trying to figure it out.
Enjoy this wonderful sky at night.

INK

Sometimes when my thoughts do wander
bizarre things I tend to ponder.
And if of this you think I jest
check this out, my latest quest.

This case in point I offer you
these idle thoughts for you to view.

Did you ever stop and think
what would we do without ink?
No written words or thoughts conveyed
by scholars on a written page.

They keep a record of histories note.
Tell stories that great minds have wrote.
We wouldn't know what Homer taught
or all the foes Achilles fought.

Shakespere, Byron, Keats and more
the list goes on score times score.
Passed down through ages year to year.
A world of words from far and near.

Thucydides wrote for all to see
but I must admit it's Greek to me.
But still it's there to read and learn
if it's his wisdom that you yearn.

It's ink that made this endeavor so
that's why I hate to see it go.

But it seems like ink might disappear
replaced by compact discs I fear.
It's Notebooks or a Kindles page
that's what now is all the rage.

Poor old ink will fade away
like Blacksmiths who outlived their day.
We'll forget important things ink's done.
Like pen the Magna Carta for one.

As I sit upon the beach one day
I find my fears are washed away.
I see that ink proliferates
but a different art form now it takes.

It's everywhere this beautiful ink
in reds and greens even shades of pink.
Its rainbow does caress the skin
so now I think that ink might win.

On legs and arms, necks and biceps
hands and ankles, wrists and triceps.
Words and pictures, there's ink galore
to see and read and adore.

It looks like ink will stay the course
not go away in sad remorse.
And now I think it's safe to say
that ink will live another day.

MY SHADOWY FRIEND

This morning early I left my home
to do my days work I would roam.
The sky was clear.
The sun was bright.
No clouds above to block the light.

Down the path onto the street
my footsteps kept a steady beat.
My heart was happy.
My spirits gay,
as I went upon my way.

A presence then I felt was there,
it was a start, a little scare.
I thought someone was at my side.
I turned abruptly to look and see,
it was my shadow stalking me.

Then I felt a trifle silly
to think my shadow gave me the willie.
I composed myself and walked once more.
I laughed and thought with some chagrin.
"You frightened me" I said to him.

My shadow didn't say a word
just kept the pace, it seemed absurd.
I couldn't loose him in a rush.
No matter how hard I tried
he was always at my side.

That is how we spent the day,
always together in work and play.
I began to think him as my friend.
He and I side by side.
He and I stride for stride.

With all the work and errands done
we turned for home again as one.
A better companion you couldn't have.
As he walked me to my door
I felt for him a grand rapport.

I went up to my room to sleep
my shadow still at my feet.
These thoughts I had as slumber came.
As I turned out the light
what does my shadow do at night?

When I snuff the candle's spark
is my shadow sleeping in the dark?

THE DUST BOWL

1930s

The old farm house weathered grey
the paint peeled long ago.
The front stoop broken, the porch roof fallen.
Earth and wind dance together on the cracked window panes.
Up soil glazed stairs, empty bedrooms.
No one calls, "Children! It's time to get up."

The old kitchen is vacant. Not quite. A rusty
iron stove, too heavy to carry away.
A cupboard door hangs, by one hinge it is saved.
Shelves bare, no goods, just the grit of time and despair.
Nude floor, not table or chair, only wear.
No one calls, "Children! Hurry, your breakfast is getting cold."

The old door frame, 'tween kitchen and parlor speaks.
Its molding molding but notched.
Intervals marking growth.
The passing of years, the shedding of tears.
Three were here.
No one calls, "Children! My, you have grown."

The old parlor window is gone. Pillaged? Salvaged?
The view is the same. Almost. Yard, fields, and now abandonment.
The fireplace won't burn, the chimney can't draw.
The mantel stolen.
Paper flowers cascade from fractured walls.
No one calls, "Children! You're under foot, go out and play."

The old screen door, screenless, bangs against the broken jam
in the endless wind, again and again and again.
Perpetual motion.
No one comes, no one goes. Maybe ghosts.
A door only in form unused in function.
No one calls, "Children! Don't slam the door."

The old oak tree bare in summer is in the yard.
A tire from a tractor or truck lies on the ground
weeds surround, reaching for the rope
where the swing once swung
and laughter once was heard.
No one calls, "Children! Come in, it's time for dinner."

The old dining room has an odor of decay
not good things to eat from a loving hand.
Mother's memories. Grandma's recipes.
Silverware tinkles, glassware sparkles.
Satisfaction, conversation.
No one calls, "Children! Finish up and do the dishes"

The old farm house once alive,
where a family lived, loved and thrived.
Day break to dark. Night to light.
Wake to rest. Sleep to sleep
now dying or died. Stark contrast to the eternal wind.
No one calls, "Children! It's time for prayer and bed."

The old farmstead now deserted. They gusted away.
Who knows to where?
Incessant, ceaseless, dust and wind, wind and dust.
No one works, no one plans, no one dreams.
No one cares.
No one calls, "Children!"

SOLDIERS! PARADE REST

A dozen flags fly in perfect harmony.
In unison on staffs spaced evenly.
Turning to and fro in the gentle breeze.
As if soldiers on parade
above this yard of the grave.
The flags are red white and blue.

The stark white stones their size exact.
In lines and rows do not detract
from those who rest beneath those stones
and the sacrifice held within their bones.
Who now mourns their loss?
We do.

The markers go on endlessly.
Farther than the eye can see.
Again as if they're on parade
to martial music only they can hear
while they sleep upon the bier.
Rest in peace.

An endless parade of the dead.
Whose blood on our behalf was shed.
If tallied they could not be counted.
In eternal sleep at last they're blessed.
Who can call the order? Soldiers! Parade Rest.
Only heaven can.

Let us not forget the best.

Rick, Mike the Irish Setter and Ginny.

TO VIRGINIA.

I remember the very last time I saw you.
I remember how you held me so tight.
You hugged me as if you knew there would be no tomorrow.
With tears on your cheek when you started to cry.
Now all that is left is my heartache and sorrow
and memories of our childhood so long ago.
The years have flown by in the blink of an eye
from the time we were children to our last goodbye.

THE BOOK OF LIFE

Like the pages of a discarded, forgotten novel
that lay in the rain and the wind.
Its pages turning slowly, by an unseen hand
one by one, never halting, from beginning to end.

Each page is a day in the life of a man
and the stories are different one from another.
What will the tale in your book tell
when you reach your last chapter, brother?

There are books of fiction and books of truth
books of hate or greed and lust.
And some of laughter and deeds of valor
and some on honor and love and trust.

A good book, like "the good book" leaves something of value
others are not worth the paper or print.
A book well written or a life well lived
synonymous both for time well spent.

U.S. CIVIL WAR

BATTLE OF GETTESBURG
THE THIRD DAY
PICKKET'S CHARGE
THE FINAL BATTLE

From far away he heard the rolling thunder
through the trees he saw the flashing of light.
All of the time he thought and did wonder
how would he do when he had to fight?

Behind the breast-work he waited and rested
with fear in his heart and sweat on his palm.
Soon the bugle would call him to be tested
against shot and shell and bullets and bomb.

Across the field he heard the cannon crackle.
All around him the shot buzzed like bees.
Hugging the ground the hair rose on his hackle
as bullets tore through the leaves on the trees.

Finally after hours a lull came to the battle
and the Sergeant advised all to lay low.
"Until you hear the sabers again rattle
and the signal to charge when the bugles blow."

In fitful sleep he lay and was dreaming
he dreamed of his friends, family and home.
He dreamed he saw his lover's eyes gleaming
and back to her arms in his dream he did roam.

He thought he was back on the farm of his father
lying beneath the apple trees that he loved.
Holding the hand of his girl, there's no other
as the breeze caressed her cheeks from above.

He remembered back when he gave her a locket
with his picture inside and a lock of his hair.
A surprise for her that he'd hid in his pocket
and it on a chain she promised she'd wear.

Shaken from slumber by the cannon fire roaring
he rose and waited for the bugle to call.
Across the field the two armies where warring
he'd go with the others to the stone wall.

Almost as one they stepped off so smartly
proud and brave and that's how they'd die.
The officer's orders rang out so sharply
outnumbered they were but they had to try.

They began to fall one by one then in numbers
first to the left and then to the right.
Fewer and fewer there were of his brothers
but on to the wall they continued to fight.

He heard the cannon, the muskets, the fighting
he heard the officers' orders so grim.
"To the stone wall that we are now sighting"
but he never heard the shot that killed him.

He died without ever firing his musket
not knowing of the war's final cost.
He went to face his final judgment
not ever knowing that their cause was lost.

Now he is home no more to face battles
buried in a grave marked by a cross.
He lies beneath a tree ripe with apples
while all who knew him mourn at his loss.

The girl is there with a bouquet of flowers
and the breeze still caresses her cheeks.
Drying her tears, she's been there for hours
and on her breast the locket she keeps.

SOPHIE'S ZITHER

On a table of others' unwanted things
it just seemed to call out to me.
An antique Zither missing some strings
only a couple, just two or three.

I took it home, I couldn't wait to begin
I couldn't wait to make the repairs.
I wanted to hear it make music again
in the hands of someone who cares.

With strings replaced and brought into tune
it hadn't been tuned in years.
I sat down to play one afternoon
oh! what music it brought to my ears.

I picked the notes and strummed the chords
it rang out so sweet and clear.
Almost as if played by another's hands
as if someone else was near.

That is when I made the find
in the box of scores which with it came.
A small white card in ink was signed.
In written hand was Sophie's name.

The card granted Sophie music lessons.
It was dated ninety-five years ago.
Twenty times she had this learning session
to help her musical knowledge grow.

Not much more than a child's toy
given to Sophie so long ago.
It must have brought her so much joy
when from it she made the music flow.

When I pick it up and I play it now
I always wonder how Sophie fared.
I feel that we are connected somehow
through this old Zither that we've shared.

That is it, that's all I have, a Zither and a name.
About her history I have no clues
not who she was or from where she came.
Of her life and time I can only muse.

THE HAWK AND THE SPARROW

A little sparrow sat on the ground
and hoped the hawk was not around.
She hoped the hawk would stay away
and let her feed in peace this day.

But that wish was not to be
as she scrounged beneath the tree.
The hawk flew circles in the sky
and spied the sparrow from up high.

A spot of brown on winter's white
as seen from Sharp-shinned's circle flight.
Sharp-shinned slowly spiraled down
to take a closer look around.

She thought that this will be the time
that I can make that sparrow mine.
With talons out and wings pulled back
with blinding speed she did attack.

The sparrow sensed the hawk was near
and sped away as in first gear.
And made it to the bush of thorns
that sheltered her from hawks and storms.

Sharp-shinned failed and flew away
to try again another day.
This game they play all winter long
until in spring Sharp-shinned is gone.

THE SCARECROW

If the scarecrow could talk what might he say?
Would his only commentary be "crows stay away?"
Or might he pontificate on issues profound
and we'd listen in awe at his wisdom so sound.

All the time wondering how can this be?
A scarecrow speaking so astutely?
By his appearance we might judge that this is absurd.
How could he speak an intelligent word?

Just look at his face, at that silly grin
at his rags held together with stitches and pin.
With straw for a brain how could he attain
a vocabulary for a conversation to sustain?

So I'm having my doubts if this whole thing is real
but the scarecrow keeps spewing his sagacious spiel.
I still think he looks as if he could not speak
but he continues undaunted to philosophize and critique.

Then he looks at me and says "I know what you're thinking
but you should not need too much more convincing.
If you listen and learn you too will discover
that you never should judge a book by its cover."

SCHOOL DAYS, COOL DAYS, GOOD OLD BROKEN RULE DAYS

It didn't take me long to see
they all were quite upset with me.
The four of them were really mad.
Nun and Priest said I was bad.
Mom and Dad were looking sad.
Nor was I a happy lad
from all the attention that I had.
All I'd done was have some fun
that's how this had all begun.
I had bent a cardinal rule
and skipped an afternoon of school.
So I stood there being cool
really young but still no fool.
Trying to look like I was sorry
for my afternoon safari.
I knew I didn't dare to say
I really didn't care as they
lambasted me with words and threats
asking if I had regrets.
The lecture had then just begun
and boy I wished it was all done.
I had a feeling I might run
flee, but that was not to be.
As they each took a turn
to express to me their deep concern.
And I was way outnumbered
as they went on unencumbered.
That is when I think I slumbered.
When my mind began to wander.
As they told me I should ponder
this deed, this youthful indiscretion
and they wanted a confession.
Were they making an impression?

From playing hooky I'd abstain
and never skip a class again.
Of course with this I did agree
because I wanted to be free.
When Monsignor did decree
"tell us what you have to say
perchance you can explain away
why it is you went astray
and went fishing for a day.
And for your sake make it good
because I want it understood
that I find some satisfaction
in punishing the least infraction."
Well, I hung my head and said
"I guess I think I was misled.
I now know that I really blew it
but the devil made me do it."
A weak excuse and I knew it.
I took a chance and took a glance
just to see how that would fly.
I heard a sigh, they wouldn't buy
the first excuse I did try.
I had to think of something new
or soon I knew I would be through.
My mind was racing to explain
and I really felt the strain
when it came just like a flame
the place where I could aim the blame.
So I blurted out the claim
"Blame it on Mark Twain."

Silence filled the room as they
looked at me with such dismay.
A puzzled look they did display
as I struggled to delay
the consequences of my deed.
At first I thought I would succeed
until the priest said, "Well, oh dear!

This I really want to hear."
I knew I was not in the clear
as above his glasses he did peer
at me as if I were a worm.
He stared at me to make me squirm.
I felt like I was in a hole
and getting deeper, out of control.
Again at them a glance I stole
and saw not one sympathetic soul.
So on I went, now on a roll.
I said "When in class a week ago
Sister asked us did we know
of a story that would show
how it must have been to grow
up in a different century
and that is when it came to me.
So I thought I'd take a look
and read that old and famous book."
Then Sister Margret Look So Stern
said "when you read and heed you learn."
"And knowing that she is so wise
and always wanting to advise.
And knowing that she will chastise
and me not wanting her reprise.
So I took a pole and hook
and went out fishing in the brook.
Instead of school that very day
the game of hooky I did play.
So she's the one that led me there
and he's the one that if I dare
say wrote the famous fabled story
said playing hooky has its glory.

Folks for ages reveled in
the tale of Tom and friend Huck Finn.
The story that Mark Twain did spin
so all this trouble starts with him."

The reverend finally called my bluff
and said "I think that we have heard enough"
and I knew that he'd be tough.
He took his glasses off his nose
and pinched the bridge as in repose.
He rubbed his temple as if in pain
then looked at me with great disdain.
He said, "I thought that I had heard it all
from when I first answered the call.
And I must say you have gall
to offer us a single word
of your story so absurd.
But in truth I have to say
that I think you've earned an A
for great effort in the way
you've tried so hard to take away
any guilt that's in your heart
or any guilt that's on your part.
And again I say if I'm allowed
I think you'd make Sam Clemens proud.
He'd surely say on your behalf
you certainly gave us all a laugh.
But now it's time to pay the price
penance for your angling vice.
And let me be yet more precise.
We gathered here have all agreed
that discipline is what you need
so retribution's guaranteed."

So I was grounded for a while
and tried to do my time in style
managing to keep a smile.
I spent my time productively
finding some activity
while in my home captivity.
My fishing tackle all came out
I fixed it up to leave no doubt
that it was all in good shape
for when I finally did escape.
The punishment I could endure
the grounding that they hope would cure
the lure of the fishing lure.
Then one fine day it was all done.
My mother said, "Well now son
a new chapter in you life's begun.
And I think in the long run
that in your mind it's now fact
that you will think before you act.
And not ditch school and waste away
your time fishing for a day."
She continued, "Now I think you ought
have learned the lesson that we sought."
As she spoke I had this thought
now that my freedom had been earned
I discerned the lesson learned.
All their effort was for naught
the next time I just won't get caught.

WHIM

I've got a yen to ride again and look like Peter Fonda
so I'll ride a pricey Harley, not no dicey Honda.
Then on my arms I'll need tattoos to prove that I'm a biker.
But for me to do that trick, they'll have to be peel and stick
cause needles make me hyper.

Then for the next step in my prep, some clothes I must acquire.
Things of black leather that go together will augment my attire.
A jacket full of pockets with shiny zippers would do the trick.
With a screaming, fierce bald eagle, on the back would look so regal
and I would look so slick.

I'll look so cool as I tool up and down the highway.
Dressed to kill, I'll ride with skill, as I leave my driveway.
Rumble, rumble here I go, my neighbors watch in awe.
Oh my gosh, I'll look so neat, as I pass them on the street
and leave them doubting what they saw.

But then I woke, it's all a joke, I think that I was dreaming.
Me on a bike, that's a hike, with leather that is gleaming.
Yes, I'm going out to take a ride, I'm going to ride again.
But you can be the one to gauge, when I ride I'll act my age
and do it on my Schwinn.

HUMMINGBIRD

I suppose some might think it is truly absurd
to cater to this smallest of bird.
For they won't let you watch them for long
and rarely if ever can you hear their song.
But that's what we do
from early spring and all summer through
and all the way into the fall.
We happily feed them all.
Their erratic flight brings such delight
to children and grandparents alike
and every single age in-between.
With smiles on our faces we take in the scene.
From feeders to flowers
they entertain us for hours
at our front porch hummingbird canteen.

THE BUTTERFLY

Drifting on a current of air
floating on a summer breeze
Touching down here and there
with a gentle grace and ease.
Drinking in the nectar golden
the harvest from the garden sweet.
From the flowers they have chosen
they take its sweet and tasty treat.
Their gossamer wings give them flight
and come in many colors true.
Allowing them to gain some height
and giving them a lofty view.
In ones and twos and sometimes threes
they frolic in the summer sun.
Playing with the honey bees
all day long they're having fun.
I envy them as they play
in my garden by and by.
And I think for just one day
I'd like to be a butterfly.

THREE FLOWERS AND A BUTTERFLY

There are three flowers on the hibiscus bush out front.
Bright red but only three.
After all it is fall in Florida.

The wind that has been a plague for days has calmed
and the sun is peeking through the clouds.
I feel its warmth on my back.

So too must the big yellow butterfly visiting the flowers.
Spending time at each one.
Spreading its wings, feeling the sun.

The sun goes behind the clouds again and the air turns cool.
The butterfly disappears, I go inside.
The flowers will be gone by morning.

The seasons come and go. The flowers blossom and die.
Time passes, we grow older.
All is fleeting.

FOOTPRINTS IN THE SNOW

If you take a walk in winter
and see your footprints in snow.
You see they only show you where you've been
never where you go.

Because no one knows the future
we just have to wait and see.
Then go forward step by step
however deep the snow might be.

So take my hand and walk with me
the dice of life we'll throw.
We'll take the journey together
and leave our footprints in the snow.

And when the snow has melted
and our footprints fade away
we'll still be together
and together we will stay.

JAVIER THE HAULER

Javier came from down south of the border
like Javier liked to say "down Mexico way".
Javier worked hard and saved his money in order
to buy an old truck and haul freight for pay.

On the door of his truck he did proudly display
JAVIER THE HAULER
NO JOB IS TOO TOUGH.
And he worked very hard, he worked night and day
taking every job he could find whether easy or rough.

Javier was known to be a man very honest
to his integrity others could not hold a candle.
A man of his word he did all that he promised
so his business grew quickly to more than he could handle.

So he bought more trucks to add to his fleet
and hired more men to work by his side.
He insisted that everything be shiny and neat
for his name on the trucks filled Javier with pride.

As the years came and went his business had grown
JAVIER THE HAULER was known far and near.
But he did not relax, he kept his nose to the stone
because in his mind his mission was clear.

HAVIER THE HAULER

Javier just wanted to be his own man.
Only owe himself for his failure or success.
And be a model to his children was Javier's plan
and he accomplished it all with humility and finesse.

After working for years Javier finally retired
and he did it with much success and acclaim.
A party was given where he was so admired
and a banner was hung honoring Javier's name.

"You are so lucky" at the party someone said
and Javier said, "Thanks, I've heard that a lot."
But in his mind Javier knew how he got ahead
it seemed the harder he worked the luckier he got.

THE PASSING

I passed the man each working day
he going his and me, my way.
For years and years he'd board the train
as I got off each day the same.
I would nod and smile at him
and he would nod and smile and then
he'd disappear in his swiftness
going about his daily business.
Although I know it seems absurd
we never exchanged a single word.
For all that time it never changed
almost as if prearranged.
I never thought to ask his name
or even ask from where he came.
Then one day he was not there
it was a start to me I swear.
Nowhere was he to be seen
our daily meeting to convene.
It stayed like that for a week or two
until one day I finally knew
that I had to face the fact.
Because our encounters had been exact
and he no longer was there each day
I knew the man had passed away.

THE DEVIL'S DARK SPACE

It's the absence of light that creates the dark
and in that dark space is where the devil lurks.
So if to his realm you chose to embark
you'll find out quite soon just how he works.

You will find that he comes in many a guise
he can look like an angel to the naïve.
But let me express a word to the wise
it's only his attempt to mislead and deceive.

His goal is to seduce with pleasure and promise
that is how he would deceive you.
You must always be a "Doubting Thomas"
when things appear too good to be true.

He tells us the easy way is the best
we should ignore such things as honor and trust.
From our soul those virtues he would like to divest
and replace them with envy, greed, self and lust.

With a great deal of deception his home looks exciting
but once you step in it's a different sight.
It really is not very pleasant or inviting
it's hot as hades and as dark as night.

You never may know when or where he'll appear
it's a life long struggle to escape from his grasp.
Ignore all his lies and his promises insincere
that's the only way to stay out of his clasp.

Look to the heavens and see the bright light
don't step through the door of the devil's inferno.
If you follow the path of goodness and right
You'll be rewarded with happiness eternal.

THE WINDS OF LOVE

Love can be like a hurricane blowing.
You never quite know which way it is going.
Just when you think all's sweet and warm.
You find it's the calm before the storm.

If you care to keep your love ship afloat.
Beware of the wind that can sink your boat.
Hold your course until the storms passed.
And if you survive your love just may last.

When all is clear and the skies are bright.
Don't drop your guard and don't lose sight.
Like any good sailor be fearful of Poseidon.
There's another storm brewing just over the horizon.

THE IRON WORKER

Up and up and up it goes
red iron against a cold grey sky.
Piece by perilous piece it grows
floor by floor it rises high.

This steel does not just fall in place
as if set by god like hands.
It must be wrestled piece by piece
by the strong, gloved hands of man.

Sunburn, windburn, cuts and scrapes
that's the price that's often paid.
Keep on going "get 'er done"
that's the motto of the trade.

How can someone do this task
this hearty job, I ask of you?
I'm proud to say I'm one of them
I'm one amongst the few.

When the building's occupied
and all are safe and sound inside.
The iron worker began it all
this truth to you I do confide.

So now that I retired
a couple years ago.
I spent my time, paid my dues
with over 40 years to show.

I really do not miss the cold
the wind and rain or snow.
But I miss my brothers in the trade
it's hard to let them go.

A TIME TO DREAM

Is there not a man who's been a boy?
Who remembers the time of youthful joy.
Of swimming fish and bounding deer
of deep dark woods and lakes so clear.

When put to bed with a loving hug
he fell asleep in his bed so snug.
Dreaming of ships and pirate lore
of sailing the main from shore to shore.

Or maybe a cowboy brave and steadfast
herding longhorns on the prairie vast.
Riding his pony on the Texas plain
tall in the saddle, his hand on the rein.

But a boy must grow up to be a man
with children of his own, that's life's grand plan.
With all the responsibility fatherhood does deem
he must always still take the time to dream.

A SNOWY DAY IN JANUARY

What a beautiful winter scene.
As pretty as a Christmas card.
Snow is on the evergreen
and blanketing the yard.

All the birds are at the feeders
Cardinals and Blue Jay.
And in the branches of the cedars
are little Juncos of black and grey.

The Chickadees are on a limb
and Sparrows scrounge around the ground.
In winter pickings can be slim
but they all know where crumbs are found.

The Woodpecker attacks a block of suet
it's frozen but he pecks away.
And he knows that he can do it
and get that tasty, fatty entrée.

And coming headfirst down the oak
the Nuthatch also waits its turn.
The Woodpecker's wrath it does not want to evoke
so it waits with some concern.

They are all there in the crisp cold air
all these birds of a feather.
Enjoying the abundance of our front yard fare
in spite of all this snowy weather.

A Halloween Poem

Ghostly shapes in the dark, dark night.
Goblins stalk my front porch light.
Witches lurking all around.
In the shadows demons abound.

I hear a noise in the rustling leaves.
Just out of sight amongst the trees.
Some kind of spook? What could it be?
I feel a chill, it frightens me.

Was that a poltergeist I saw?
A monster with a gruesome claw?
Or just a figment of my fear.
I just don't know, it's so unclear.

There's witches and goblins and ghosts galore.
And they're quite impossible to ignore.
They all call out for me to hear.
Unpleasant, annoying to my ear.

All at once on me it dawned.
Of these beings the night has spawned.
It must be that time of year.
When apparitions do appear.

I'll invite them in, into the light.
See what they want, ignore my fright.
They seem so happy, playful, merry.
Perhaps they're really not so scary.

They come in close with hands outstretched.
Bright faces on which smiles are etched.
All they want is a simple treat.
A little gift, a sweet to eat.

A trick I do want to prevent.
A deed intended to torment.
So I pass around the candy bowl.
And so it seems that does console.

Then off they go into the night.
Back to the dark and out of sight.
They fade again to things unseen.
And from the dark they call "Happy Halloween."

DAPHNE DU MAURIER

I asked of Daphne du Maurier one day
"please, Daphne would you marry me?"
She replied, "Dear boy you know I can't.
Your sweet request I cannot grant."

I felt as if my heart were trampled
as the pain inside I sampled.
I asked her if she would explain
in hopes that that might ease my pain.

"You see," she said, "There's reasons three.
The first to change my name would be
a trifle short of travesty.
Because
my name's so grand and yours mundane
so I must keep my name the same."

On my knees again I spoke to her
and said,
"Your point of view I could concur.
If to take my name you are adverse
we could do the name change in reverse."

The nuptial vows we'd rearrange
my name to hers I would change.
Then
to the world I'd be known as Mr. Daphne
and once that's done we'd both be happy.

Or
how about maybe to Rick du Maurier
that certainly has a certain play.
She could pick one of the two
either way if she'd say I do.

I hoped to ease her dissatisfaction
as I awaited her reaction.
She finally said, "Oh my, I'm still in doubt
there are other things to think about."

"You forget that I'm already wed
to the man I lovingly call Fred.
And I would surely be remiss
if indeed I let you steal a kiss."

So I asked,
"And what pray tell is number three
tell me please what that would be?"
My spirits had begun to slide
for I knew she would not be my bride.

Again she spoke,
"You see, there's such a difference in our ages
and you only know me through the pages.
You only know of HILLS and BIRDS
or JAMAICA INN, in other words
you only know my books and prose
we've never met and heaven knows
I'm older by a generation
but flattered by your infatuation."

Like a bomb it all became quite certain
on my wish she'd pulled the final curtain.
But other things became unclear.
Like, am I there or is she here?

Well, I am here.
I've been sitting in my lounging chair
reading her novel THE WINDING STAIR.
And I realized I'd been dozing.
Dreaming all I'd been proposing.

For years I've read all she had written
and guess that's why I am so smitten.
I love her literary repertoire
but I have to love her from afar.

Well, love is won and love is lost
as on a windswept sea it's tossed.
Blown here or blown there
so you might find it anywhere.

DUCKS IN A ROW

I'm a pretty organized guy.
I like to keep my ducks in a row.
It's better not to just let them fly
all willy nilly and to and fro.

But if you're a duck it's often said
"watch out for anyone with a gun."
So with that said my ducks fly in dread
and refuse to walk in a row one by one.

They simply just won't stay in line
because someone's always taking a shot.
They like to scatter, these ducks of mine
almost as if there's some kind of a plot.

I really can't blame them for if it were I
if I were a duck and the table was turned
I'd be the first to run, flee or fly
because of all the lessons I've learned.

A potshot here or a potshot there
I guess in the end it's all up to luck.
But with potshots coming from everywhere
I'm still trying to teach my ducks to duck.

And I have to say that although
I've paid them all a hefty salary.
It's hard to keep my ducks in a row
when you're living in a shooting gallery.

A PEN IN HAND

At the pearly gates of heaven,
Saint Peter sat behind his desk.
All that wish to gain admission,
must first stand and pass his test.

A lovely lady stood before him,
with many years of life to claim.
She sought to enter heaven's gate,
Saint Peter asked her for her name.

She bowed her head and answered him,
she told him who she'd been In life.
In his book he found her page,
a friend, a mother, a loving wife.

Her face was like an angel's face,
Saint Peter said, "sweet lady dear.
It appears that you have lived so well,
to gain admission you need not fear."

"But first I must go down the list,
just bear with me until I'm done."
He took his quill pin from his desk
and started checking one by one.

"Just a thing that I must do,
let me quickly check your record."
Down the list he quickly flew,
checking if her past was checkered.

The list of items was the standard.
"Did you lie or steal a thing?
Is there one you might have slandered?
Did in anger your tongue sting?"

On and on Saint Peter went,
until it seemed that he was done.
O're the list his head was bent
and imperfections he found none.

"Well what is this?" Saint Peter asked.
As a note fell from the book.
St Peter read it and was aghast
and a deep breath then he took.

"Tell me all about the pens.
The ones for years that you have taken.
I guess it does not seem like sins
but I assure you you're mistaken."

She seemed sincere in her sweetness
as on she spoke, her tale to tell.
"Oh, I know it is my weakness,
a pen in hand that writes so well."

"All my life I've loved to write
and most pens are a pain you know.
So when I find one that's alright,
I just can't stand to let it go."

"And besides the ones in question,
are in the motels just to take.
It seems so small an indiscretion,
of all the heavenly rules to break."

"And I think you do agree,
for I see the way you hold your quill.
I think that you must feel like me.
You understand a good pen's thrill."

St Peter had to stop and think,
he understood just what she meant.
He loved his quill pen and its ink
and so he knew he must relent.

"I guess that I can understand
but I'm sure that you knew,
to take those pen for your hand
would cause some penance for you to do."

"So write for me on this paper,
that you repent for your deed.
And you are sorry for the caper,
then give it back to me to read."

A little smile lit up her face
and she sweetly said. "Well then.
Thank you for your forgiving grace
and may I please use your pen?"

AN EVENING IN THE WOODS

I'm sitting outside on a warm summer night,
watching the moon rise and the stars twinkle bright.
It makes me feel good, it just all feels so right,
all I see and hear on this warm summer night.

All of my cares just drift away
as I sit with my fiddle, so relaxed as I play.
The musical notes join the bats on the wing
and as I play I listen and I hear them sing.

From out by the pond next to the forest
the frogs have joined in singing the chorus.
A robin chirp, chirps announcing the dark
and off in the distance I hear a dog bark.

From somewhere above in the waning light,
geese are honking in homeward flight.
Adding the base as they also join in,
baritone accompaniment to my violin.

There are crickets and toads and an occasional crow
all joined together to put on this show.
All joined together in this nocturnal company.
All joined together in this back yard symphony.

And I am so privileged to be the conductor
but it is all the critters that are the instructor.
I get the message as they all sing together,
when we all work as one things turn out for the better.

CHASING THE WHALE

The lookout sings out, "there she blows."
Now the chase begins.
The master calls out, "hard to port.
Bring her closer to the wind."

The rigging groans as the stays are stretched
and the old ship picks up speed.
All eyes scan for the water spouts,
the creature's course we need.

Hull down the rail is in the foam,
foam from the ice cold sea.
The decks awash. The scoffers pour
but the pod proceeds to flee.

Get close enough to launch the boats.
Fill the hold with oil.
That's what this is all about,
this hunt, this whaler's toil.

The whales swim straight and stay their course,
while we must tack to gain.
They don't even know that we are here.
It seems we chase in vain.

For almost 15 hours now
the pod has swum as one.
We haven't gained a single league,
this time the beast has won.

And so it is this whaler's way
yet it's the way I choose.
You work so hard and risk your life.
Sometimes you win, but most you lose.

LIMERICK TO A JUNK MAN

I derive so much pleasure, in finding some treasure,
in another man's discarded trash.
Some of things, I keep for myself and display on a shelf,
the remainder I sell for some cash.

It is the truth, that back in my youth,
I was up and out early without delay.
The original recycler, the adolescent bicycler,
towing my wagon on pick up day.

I still have that desire, for junk to acquire,
this passion never will cease.
I can't shake the urge, of a junk pile to purge,
and bring home, piece after piece.

My wife shakes her head in dismay, when I proudly display,
my latest salvaging find.
Then she warms to the fact, that it's just part of my act,
and to that she now is resigned.

So that's how it goes and only heaven knows,
what next I will bring into our home.
But you can be sure, I'm an entrepreneur,
every time the streets I do roam.

LOVE'S FAIR WIND

Driven by the autumn wind
the ship of sails brings him home.
He's roamed the world from end to end
but now no longer will he roam.

Across the waves the wind blows fair
as the sun sinks in the west.
The scent of home is in the air.
This voyage will be his final quest.

It's said the test of time love stands.
He wonders as he rides the swell.
He's been to all those foreign lands
and soon the test of time will tell.

The wind born spray stings his eyes
and causes them to tear.
From high above a sea bird cries
sharing in his fear.

From high atop a swaying mast
through the long spy glass he gazes.
He thinks of her and his heart beats fast,
remembering all of loves sweet phrases.

Vows exchanged between two lovers,
two years and more they've been apart.
They promised that they'd see no others
and hold each other in their heart.

But two years can be a time too long.
Too long to ask someone to wait.
A time when memories are gone.
This thought he had as the bell struck eight.

Across the rolling sea they ply
when he heard the call. "Land ho."
On the line between sea and sky
a spot of land began to show.

Onward, onward plows the ship.
Closer, closer to the shore.
Almost time to end this trip
and be away from her no more.

At the wharf with the ship secure
he leans against the rail so weathered.
Still not knowing, still unsure
if their hearts are truly tethered.

In the crowd of smiling faces
welcoming those gone so long.
There she stands in all her graces,
his heart is filled with joy and song.

With his duffel on his shoulder
he hurries down the wooden plank.
He can hardly wait to hold her.
He knows that he has God to thank.

All his doubts are washed away
as they hold each other tight.
Her love for him her eyes betray
as love's sweet phrases they again recite.

Life and love are oft depending
as to what is in the air.
And there can be a happy ending,
when the winds of love blow fair.

ORION THE HUNTER

It is the time of year that winter draws near
and a cold wind starts to blow from the north.
As the sun says farewell, our memory might dwell,
on autumn and its color and warmth.

That north wind can be shrill when it brings a chill
and the nights grow longer and colder by far.
It brings the clear sky of winter when the weather is bitter
and the hunter with his bright belted star.

In his bow there's an arch as he starts his march,
each evening across the crisp sky.
A celestial odyssey in the world of astronomy,
he is quite a star studded guy.

Night after night, what a magnificent sight,
as undaunted he trudges along.
Ever onward the archer, the persistent marcher,
until one night in spring he'll be gone.

But you can count on that fact that he will be back,
like clockwork again in the fall.
So dependable is he, I think you'd agree,
he's the greatest constellation of them all.

OUR GARDEN

What on this earth does more blessings bestow
than a garden in abundance where flowers do grow?
We love our garden all through the year
but it's in the summer that it brings the most cheer.

With sunflowers and coneflowers and zinnias and impatience
all growing together and looking so gracious.
Roses and butterfly bushes and flowers,
they all bring us much pleasure for hours and hours.

And it's not only us that hold this garden dear.
Once it's in bloom other admirers appear.
Butterflies and bees and humming birds abound
and ladybugs and moths, they all come around.

Its fragrance permeates the warm summer air.
With a plethora of colors from its pallet to share.
It's a miracle of nature to watch it unfold.
A miracle of nature for us all to behold.

This magnificent sight grows right into the fall.
Sharing its beauty with one and all.
Until in the winter it will all disappear.
Leaving only a memory 'til we start over next year.

REFLECTIONS

I looked into the mirror to see what I could see
but I didn't recognize the face looking back at me.
I couldn't find the boy with that optimistic smile.
Well, now that I think of it, I hadn't seen him in awhile.

A fact about a mirror is it always tells the truth.
That's why I can't find the reflection of my youth.
The image that I see is what is really there.
In the glare from the mirror we are a bookend pair.

I see an older man, his brow furrowed with concern.
His reflection telling me that the boy cannot return.
Maturity and age is what has brought the change
but I have to wonder if it was a fair exchange.

It's life's trials and tribulations for which we pay a price.
If you doubt what I'm saying let me be yet more precise.
If you dare to take a chance go look into a mirror.
Then the reflection looking back at you will make it all so clear.

SPINNING OUT OF CONTROL

Spin around like a top
then close your eyes until you stop.
Open them and see what's there.
War is brewing everywhere.

Hungry children left unfed.
Mothers who are filled with dread.
How does she help them to survive?
How does she help them stay alive?

Orphans with no place to go.
War has always made it so.
The children always suffer much
when they feel its hateful touch.

Mostly waged for political gain
or religious fervor that seems insane.
Truly mankind's greatest folly.
The bullets fly in a volley.

Indiscriminate as to what they peril,
news reels make it look so sterile.
Unleash the bombs and let them fall,
young and old just kill them all.

Can we ever stop the waste?
Civilization's huge disgrace.
I wonder if it could be done,
to unite the world to be as one?

Let's let the children rule the earth.
Without preconceptions at their birth,
they know no prejudice or hate,
too bad adults can't share that trait.

Watch them in a nursery school
as they learn the golden rule.
With one another they have no fear.
With one another they do cohere.

Reverse the roles is what I say.
Let their innocence hold sway.
Put them in charge to be the leaders.
Let the children be the teachers.

STUCK IN THE CAR WASH BLUES

I was filling up with gas on an ice cold winter day
when the gas pump asked, "do you want a wash today?"
I thought why not I'll just rinse the salt away.
Little did I know I'd be in that wash to stay.

I pulled up to the door and quickly put in my token,
never even thinking the machine might be broken.
But once inside, the exit door wouldn't open.
Out of frustration some expletives were spoken.

I tried to back on up and get on out of there
but the door was still stuck, I wasn't going anywhere.
I was tiring very fast of this whole bizarre affair.
Thinking the time had come to recite the Lord's Prayer.

Backward and forward, time and time I did try.
Without much success, I thought I must surely die.
They will find me in spring with many months gone by.
Well, my car will sure be clean when my friends all say goodbye.

One last time I would try to garner my release,
before I called 911 to summon the police.
There has to be a way, this nonsense has to cease.
The longer this went on my anxiety did increase.

Finally I was able to crawl out my driver's door,
amidst the dripping brushes and the dirt upon the floor.
I squeezed out of an opening, finally free once more
and headed to the store, some help I would implore.

I was standing in the line the lady giving me the eye,
very cold and wet and trying to get dry.
As I started to explain how things had gone awry,
she raised her hand and said, "hold it, just standby."

She summoned the attendant to come and talk to me
and when I had explained he said, "let's take a look and see."
When he saw the problem, he shrugged and did decree.
"You never use this wash at this cold of degree."

So I stood there shaking and feeling rather dumb,
for listening to the gas pump, its offer to succumb.
Still cold and wet, my hands and feet were numb.
Well, I've learned to let my car stay dirty until spring
has finally come.

THE LONELY SAILOR

Oh! Don't come a calling you lonely young seaman.
Just stay far away like your dreams unfulfilled.
You have no future as a merchant marine man.
You will die poor and broken or at best just be killed.

You have nothing to offer this lady of standing.
How could she ever fit into your life?
She's genteel and cultured, so different from you man.
She could never be happy if she were your wife.

You've seen the worst that the world has to offer.
You've fought tooth and nail just to survive.
She's never experienced so frightful a life style.
While you are so lucky to just be alive.

So take the next ship heading out to the ocean.
Take the next ship going out on the sea.
Seek out and ask the old bearded boatswain,
"as a sailor of ships is this meant to be?"

Then sail out on the vast empty waters.
Long for horizons you never can reach.
Slumber at night as the waves rock you gently
and dream of the girl whose love you beseech.